DAD JOKES

POCKET-SIZED

BEN THOMAS

ISBN-10: 1981614427
ISBN-13: 978-1981614424

Q. **Why was the skeleton making jokes?**

A. *He was trying tibia little humerus!*

Q. **Why should you be suspicious of trees?**

A. *They're very shady!*

Q. **Why didn't the dad buy camouflage pants?**

A. *He couldn't find any!*

Q. **What happened to the frog's car?**

A. *It got toad!*

Q. **What are ninja's favourite type of shoes?**

A. *Sneakers!*

Q. **What's orange and sounds like a parrot?**

A. *A carrot!*

Q. Why shouldn't you feed teddy bears?

A. *They're already stuffed!*

Q. What happened when the dad tried to punch a patch of fog?

A. *He mist!*

Q. **Why did the irritable doctor get fired?**

A. *He lost his patients!*

Q. **Why did the dad wear his glasses to the math test?**

A. *It improves devision!*

Q. How do snails fight?

A. *They slug it out!*

Q. What do you call a snowman that doesn't tell the truth?

A. *A snow fake!*

To steal ideas from one person is plagiarism..

To steal from many is research!

Q. **What does reading while sunbathing make you?**

A. *Well red!*

Q. Why did the dad get fired from his job at the orange juice factory?

A. *He couldn't concentrate!*

Q. Did you hear about the guy whose whole left side got cut off?

A. *He's all right now!*

Q. What's red and bad
for your teeth?

A. *A brick!*

Q. What happened to
the sick Italian chef?

A. *He pasta-way!*

Q. **What is a mummies favourite genre of music?**

A. *Wrap music!*

Q. **How do you feel when you run out of coffee?**

A. *Depresso*

Q. What happened to the dyslexic Satanist?

A. *He worshiped Santa!*

My doctor told me I was crazy, so I said that I wanted a second opinion..

He said okay, you're stupid too!

You spend the first 2 years teaching children to walk and talk..

then the next 16 years telling them to sit down and shut-up!

Q. **If Santa rides in a sleigh, what do elves ride in?**

A. *Mini vans!*

Q. Where can you find
birthday presents
for cats?

A. *In a cat-alogue!*

Q. Why do trees love spring?

A. *It's a re-leaf!*

Q. What did the nut say
when it was chasing
the other nut?

A. *I'm a cashew!*

Q. Why couldn't the
dad find his map?

A. *Because he lost his map.*

Q. What did the person who invented the knock knock joke win?

A. *The Nobel prize!*

Q. Which side of a chicken has the most feathers?

A. *The outside!*

Q. Why can't a nose
be 12 inches long?

A. *Because then it
would be a foot!*

Q. What do you call a
guy who is leaving
a hospital?

A. *Manuel!*

Q. **Why didn't anybody want to eat the crushed Tic Tac?**

A. *It was no longer in mint condition!*

Q. **Who is Frosty the snowman's favorite Aunt?**

A. *Aunt Artica!*

They say you're
not supposed to
eat at night..

*but then why is there
a light bulb in the
refrigerator?*

Q. **What tea do soccer
players drink?**

A. *Penaltea!*

Q. Why are pilots
always nervous?

A. *Their jobs are always
up in the air!*

Q. What do you call a
railroad apprentice?

A. *A trainee!*

Q. How did the dad become a vegetarian?

A. *He quit cold turkey!*

Q. What does a clock do when it's hungry?

A. *It goes back four seconds!*

Q. **Why did the dad play soccer even though he was terrible at it?**

A. *For the kicks!*

Q. **Why do gorillas have big nostrils?**

A. *Because they have big fingers!*

Some people create happiness wherever they go..

others create happiness whenever they go!

Where does mistletoe go to find fame?

Holly-wood!

Q. **What would bears be without bees?**

A. *Ears!*

Q. **What do you call a man with a rubber toe?**

A. *Roberto!*

Q. What's red and smells like blue paint?

A. *Red Paint!*

I was an ATM and an old lady asked me to help check her balance..

so I pushed her over!

Q. **Why are Army clothes always so tired?**

A. *Because they're fatigues!*

Q. **What do Alexander the Great and Winnie the Pooh have in common?**

A. *The same middle name!*

Q. What do you call a
can opener that
doesn't work?

A. *A can't opener!*

Q. Why should you
never write with
a dull pencil?

A. *Because it's pointless.*

Q. **What are a snowman's favorite two letters of the alphabet?**

A. *I C!*

I bought a vacuum cleaner six months ago..

so far all it's been doing is gathering dust!

Q. **Why do birds fly south for the winter?**

A. *Because its too far to walk!*

Q. **What do you call a person without a body or a nose?**

A. *Nobody knows!*

Q. **What happened to the dad who fell in love during a backflip?**

A. *He was heels over head!*

Q. **What was the only thing left after the French cheese factory exploded?**

A. *De Brie!*

Q. Why should you never
lie to an x-ray technician?

A. *They can see right
through you!*

Q. Why do you never
see elephants
hiding in trees?

A. *Because they're
so good at it!*

Q. **Why shouldn't you buy anything made of Velcro?**

A. *Because it's a rip-off!*

Q. **How did Luke Skywalker get to the shop?**

A. *Ewoked!*

**People assume I'm a
vegetarian because
I love animals..**

*but it's actually
because I hate plants!*

Q. **What's the difference
between a cookie
and an elephant?**

A. *You can't dunk an
elephant in your tea!*

Q. Who lives at the North Pole, makes toys and travels around in a pumpkin?

A. *Cinder-elf-a!*

Q. How did the butcher introduce his wife?

A. *Meet Pattie!*

Q. What happened at the emotional wedding?

A. *The cake was in tiers!*

Q. Why did the foul-mouthed nun get expelled?

A. *Because of her dirty habit!*

Q. **What did the dad say when the sink was full of dirty plates?**

A. *Dishes a real mess!*

Q. **Why does Waldo wear a striped shirt?**

A. *Because he doesn't want to be spotted!*

Q. **Why was the broom late for work?**

A. *It overswept!*

Q. **How many tickles does it take to make an octopus laugh?**

A. *Ten-tickles!*

**Apparently I snore
so loudly..**

*that it scares everyone
in the car I'm driving!*

Q. **Why did Cinderella
get kicked off the
soccer team?**

A. *Because she kept
running from the ball!*

Q. **When does a lion have a trunk?**

A. *When he goes on vacation!*

Q. **How does a penguin build its house?**

A. *Igloos it together!*

Q. What do you call a
baby monkey?

A. *A chimp off the old block!*

Q. What did the slow
tomato say to the
quick tomato?

A. *I'll ketch up!*

My therapist says I'm obsessed with vengeance..

We'll see about that..

Q. **Who takes the second shot in a game of snooker?**

A. *Find out after the break!*

Q. Why does lightning
shock people?

A. *It doesn't know how
to conduct itself!*

Q. What kind of trees
do fingers grow on?

A. *Palm Trees!*

Q. What do sea captains use amphibians for?

A. *As froghorns!*

Q. Why do novice pirates make terrible singers?

A. *Because they can't hit the high seas!*

Q. **What illness do Chinese martial artist get?**

A. *Kung-flu!*

Q. **What does a baby computer call his father?**

A. *Data!*

Q. What's the difference between an African elephant and an Indian elephant?

A. *About 5000 miles!*

Q. What do you call a short psychic who has escaped from jail?

A. *A small medium at large!*

Q. **What kind of candy is never on time?**

A. *Choco-late!*

Brains aren't everything..

in some people's cases, they're nothing!

Q. What do you get when you cross Frosty the Snowman with a baker?

A. *Frosty the Dough-man!*

Q. What's the worst thing about sleeping like a log?

A. *Waking up in the fireplace!*

Q. **What does a vegetarian zombie say?**

A. *Grrraaains!*

Q. **Why do dads love jokes about sausages?**

A. *They're the wurst!*

Q. **Why didn't the gun have a job?**

A. *He got fired!*

I like long walks..

especially when they're taken by people I don't like!

Q. **What is Count Dracula's favorite Christmas story?**

A. *The fright before Christmas!*

Q. **What did the shy pebble wish for?**

A. *To be a little boulder!*

Q. **What do you call a monkey in a minefield?**

A. *A baboom!*

Q. **Did you hear about the kidnapping at the school?**

A. *It was okay, he woke up!*

Q. **What lies at the bottom of the ocean and twitches?**

A. *A nervous wreck!*

Q. **What kind of magic do cows believe in?**

A. *Moodoo!*

Q. Why couldn't the bicycle stand up by itself?

A. *It was two tired!*

Q. What kind of photos do turtles take?

A. *Shellfies!*

My doctor said that jogging could add years to my life. He was right..

I feel ten years older already!

Q. **What do you call an acid that's being unfriendly?**

A. *Amino Acid!*

Q. What do you call
a rabbit with fleas?

A. *Bugs Bunny!*

Q. Why did the cold dad
sit in the corner?

A. *Because it was 90 degrees!*

Q. Why don't cannibals eat clowns?

A. *Because they taste funny!*

Q. Why are rivers always so rich?

A. *Because they have two banks!*

Q. **What do you get if you cross Santa with a duck?**

A. *A Christmas Quacker!*

Q. **Why was the archaeologist depressed?**

A. *His career was in ruins!*

I think my employer must
have picked me for my
motivational skills..

*everyone always says they
work twice as hard when
I'm around!*

O.   **Why do ghosts
like elevators?**

A.   *Because they lift
their spirits!*

Q. What do you get if you drop a piano down a mine shaft?

A. *A flat miner!*

Q. What do you call a fake noodle?

A. *An impasta!*

Q. **Why doesn't Dracula have many friends?**

A. *Because he's a pain in the neck!*

When documents ask who is to be notified in case of an emergency..

I always write, "A very good doctor"!

Q. Why should you never make too many cookies at once?

A. *Too big of a whisk!*

My boss asked me to attach two pieces of wood together..

I nailed it!

Q. **What do you call a sleepwalking nun?**

A. *A roamin' Catholic!*

Q. **Why did the orange stop rolling down the hill?**

A. *Because it ran out of juice!*

Q. **Why couldn't the Australian general win the war on bread?**

A. *Because it was stale, mate!*

People say I look like I'm approaching forty..

but they're never sure from which direction!

**I'm planning to
live forever..**

so far, so good!

Q. **What happened when
the talented thief
joined the theatre?**

A. *He stole the spotlight!*

Q. What did the number 8 say to the 0?

A. *Do you like my belt?*

Q. Why is it so cold at Christmas?

A. *Because it's Decembrrrrr!*

My doctor said I'm only allowed to eat tropical fruit from now on..

It's enough to make a mango crazy!

Q. **What did the overly excited gardener do when spring finally arrived?**

A. *He wet his plants!*

Q. **What did the dad who had bills to pay do?**

A. *He gave it back, Bill looked silly without it!*

Q. **What did sushi A say to sushi B?**

A. *Wasa-b!*

Q. What's slow, large, grey and doesn't matter?

A. *An irrelephant!*

Q. Why should you never trust a person when they're using graph paper?

A. *They might be plotting something!*

Made in the USA
Lexington, KY
16 December 2018